Healing prayers

Stefka Harp

Healing prayers
© Stefka Mladenova 2019

All rights reserved. No part of this publication may be reproduced, stored in a retrieval system, or transmitted in any form or by any means, electronic, mechanical, photocopying, recording or otherwise, without the prior written permission of the author.

National Library of Australia Cataloguing Statement:

 A catalogue record for this book is available from the National Library of Australia

ISBN: 9780648405504

Published with the assistance of www.wordwrightediting.com.au

Images courtesy of clker.com and bigstockphotos.com.

www.stefkaharp.com

Healing prayers

Contents

Acknowledgements..v

Dedication..vi

Introduction vii

Heavenly father..1

You are Almighty 2

Love and live..3

Forgive our trespasses..4

As we forgive others 6

Holy Spirit within hear us 8

I pray for a healing..10

Prayer heals and restores 12

My personal Divine healing prayer.....................14

A powerful group healing prayer........................16

A healing prayer for the world 18

Divine healing received with grace.....................20

Gratitude for the Divine healing 22

Loving thought restores health..........................24

The Word is love..26

Health prayer 27

Graceful healing upon you and me....................28

I rejoice in the restored health 30

I love the Father, the Son and the Holy Spirit....32

Prayer for a healthy body 34
The Lord's Divine prayer 36
I love my enemies prayer 38
I desire Divine healing to find 40
Prayers are powerful 42
At the end of the day 44
Rejuvenation prayer 46
Graceful healing 48
Good night prayer 49
I send out a healing prayer every day 50
About the author 52

Acknowledgements

I wish to express my deep and sincere gratitude to my parents for teaching me the value of life — how to love and be happy as well as show kindness; and to my siblings, for being a part of my life.

My thanks, too, to the Australian Government for opening the door for me to migrate and become a permanent resident; to experience a different kind of life, culture and customs, which has been very enriching, enlightening and eye-opening. I am very grateful for the opportunity I have been given and guided to get to the point I am at.

Sincere gratitude to:

- my daughter for her patience and loving assistance in proofreading my work
- Gail, publishing advisor for the guidance given.

Dedication

Everything I write and have written so far is dedicated to the Almighty who has guided me through life without me being aware. At times my ignorance and oblivion to the facts revealed have led to strife and suffering. But these experiences have given me the much-needed fuel for my writings, and I hope they will help others. Life is like a jigsaw puzzle. Some things are meant to happen so that the pieces fit within the puzzle and we come to know the truth. Also gratitude to my parents for bringing me to this world and giving me much needed love and care, as well as gratitude to the rest of my family for being part of my life.

S.H.

Disclaimer: The author is expressing beliefs and views based on her life experience. There is no intention to offend anyone who has contrary views. The poems are fun to read and in the process can bring a positive and loving attitude.

Introduction

Any shape or form of prayers are powerful. Powerful enough to bring what is prayed for. Hopefully, a positive attitude will manifest goodness in people's lives.

I make sure my prayers reflect love and kindness, hope and faith to better myself. It is not fruitful to dwell on the negative and destructive. It is energy wasted to bring more suffering and destruction.

As with my other poems already published, *Healing prayers* are structured around good and beneficial thoughts and words that bring healing and happiness. If the poems are read more often, with time, the energy will increase and be powerful enough to yield a fruitful outcome.

I would also like to take this opportunity to add a little bit about the introduction to my previous book, *Our thoughts and words*, about the gussy wiggle that snaked over me and went through the wall.

Two weeks after my realisation of what the gussy wiggle was, I had a dream. In the dream, I could see the cloudy gray wiggle clearly in the distance, hovering over a field. Then it started breaking apart and hundreds of deadly snakes emerged and went in all directions.

I woke up wondering what the meaning of the dream was. The answer came very quickly. Other people's energy that I had been sending back to them had reached its target, and was branching off to find every individual that the energy belonged to. I became more and more convinced that thought energy is very powerful, powerful enough to make or break a person.

Stefka Harp

Healing prayers

Hearty request I implore
Ever so health to restore,
Avalanche of healing on the count of four,
Very real your outpour.
Engulfed I am in loving energy,
Necessary to be pain free,
Lifelong commitment clearly
Yielding peace and harmony.

Focused I am on my health
Amazingly, it is my wealth.
Therefore I ask to be, through a prayer,
Hassle free. I affirm with care,
Eagerly to come to me today,
Rejuvenating body and brain night and day.

Yea or nay, I take my chance.
Only you can allow at a glance, to
Undo the wrong and make me dance.

Answer my plea, Almighty you,
Reward me on the count of two with
Everlasting boundless health through and through.

Always and forever, without doubt,
Leaping and skipping over the clouds.
Merrily I go around,
Invigorated, restored and crowned.
Goodness me, I am alive
Health overflowing I find,
Timeless pure thoughts aligned, in a
Youthful body ever so Divine.

Healing prayers

Long time ago, I assigned
One time to train body and mind,
Vibrantly to relax and reflect, on
Every thought I project.

Ascertained that body and mind at best
Namely go in a state of rest,
Displaying slow rhythm in the chest.

Lovely heart and soul so dear
Instantly benefiting is clear,
Vanishing stress and fear
Enough for enjoyment to appear.

Stefka Harp

For all I know you are the
Only one who forgives in earnest,
Reassuring us to profess
Gracious kindness to impress,
Inkling to inspire at our best
Vitality to transpire and bless,
Effort worth the while for success.

Obediently, I forgive as well,
Unconditionally, those that trespass and tell
Rather against me and farewell.

Therefore I go free,
Redeeming myself with a plea,
Elevating soul Divine and
Seeking forgiveness on the count of five.
Patiently nullifying with time, when
Another undesirable thought is revealed,
Secretly hoping to be healed,
Sufficient to know and feel. The
Expectation fulfilled, unifying
Swiftly with the glory sublime.

Attention I pay to my thoughts, I
Safeguard turning them into words.

Wonders in view by dusk,
Earthly wisdom to pursue in earnest.

Forgiveness through and through,
Obvious and true, to
Restore faith in the Divine within.
Grateful I am here in, for
Inner peace to begin,
Vision of mine fulfilled by dawn,
Earnestly illness subdued and gone.

Occasion to rejoice and assert,
Triumphant I am for my effort,
Here on to forgive and spiritually grow
Energy and healing to flow. I
Rise high and touch the sky,
Splendid way to purify.

Holy Spirit within,
Outshine and be keen,
Lovingly hear us
Yes, expectation to surpass.

Soul and body needs to heal,
Purge the bad energy at will
In its entirety, until I
Rectify the wrong that brought the ill,
Immediately to be underway
Thus bringing relief in every way.

Waning, the ill symptoms go,
Invigorating body and mind to overflow, with
Thoughts that heal and restore
Healthy attitude galore,
Invoking serenity in us to feel, know and love, and
Never to lose sight of all the above.

Healing prayers

Holy Spirit hear us, we plead with you, you are the
Essence of our life, it's true!
Always there to come through
Responding gracefully without ado. You

Understand our need, so grant our plea
Soul Divine, proceed with speed.

Stefka Harp

I persistently pray,

Paramount it is to do every day,
Repent I do, and ask for healing.
At long last I get the feeling,
Yearning for good health while appealing.

First of all I give thanks and praise
On with the healing at a pace, to
Restore body and mind and amaze. I am

Healing prayers

Always keen

Healing to find herein,
Essential for the Divine spirit within.
Affectionately I desire to be healed,
Lovingly protected by a Divine Shield.
Illumination upon me to be thrilled,
Numerous times over to excel,
Gracious way illness to farewell.

Stefka Harp

Pure thoughts of well wishing I hold dear,
Ray of hope I revere,
Ample health to domineer,
Youthful body to re-appear,
Empowering me to persevere,
Renewed body and soul to cheer.

Heartfelt prayer with universal love combined,
Energy flow already aligned,
Apparently it is to remind me
Lovingly to be kind,
Sufficient healing to find.

Healing prayers

Aspects I do not dismiss
Now and forever, I persist,
Dynamic thought energy to assist.

Realistically forgiveness is the clue,
Ever so powerful to undo,
Seemingly negative energy to subdue
Thus casting out the residue.
On with the new thinking,
Revealing the Divine is leading,
Eternally aiming,
Swiftly to reflect the Holy Spirit within.

Minute to have, moment to spare, I always
Yearn for the Divine energy to flare, I

Plead with you, Father, that you care,
Earnestly your name I call in prayer.
Remove errors and open the way,
Swiftly channel Divine energy without delay
Over and through my body as you may,
Nightly to be underway
And any time in between I pray, as a
Loving father does every day.

Divine energy
Is flowing definitely,
Vigorously to heal body and heart,
It's on the way to depart
Notably from the tip of my toes, healing
Energy to the top of my head flows.

Healing prayers

Harmonious warmth radiates from my core,
Enormously that heals and restores,
Allowing body and soul to glow,
Love Divine to bestow,
Infinitely, for all I know.
Nevertheless, I am adamant,
Graciously to drink from the holiest fountain.

Permeating body, heart and soul,
Rejuvenation to thrill is my goal,
As I trust I have been healed,
Your invisible healing power revealed, I
Express gratitude with all my heart,
Renewed body and soul is a start.

Allow us (insert name) to pray for you,

Possibilities are endless with the Divine.
Out we go and plead with the spirit within,
Well and truly to come through herein
Eagerly, as the Almighty knows how, to
Remedy what's been lost.
Feel healing energy flowing foremost,
Unwanted illness cast out,
Lovingly what we seek is your turnabout.

Generous person you are, it's true,
Resourceful and willing to give a helping hand, as
Often as you can. In an
Unselfish way, you always assist,
Passionate to the core to say the least.

Healing we ask for, so sit back and relax,
Earthly prayers endorsed with love to grasp.
Amazingly, with your permission, at long last,
Lo and behold, we nullify the energy around you,
Instantly, that brought the illness through,
Never to return, ever again.
Gratitude to the Divine in your name.

Healing prayers

Peace loving nature we admire,
Restoration of your body we insist to transpire,
All the way, from the tips of your toes
Yes, to the top of your head energy flows,
Energy heals and restores, feel it again and again
Rejoice in restored health in God's name.

(One person reads a line then the group repeats it)

This poem was written to honour my friends Jean, Myra and Brenda, members of the Salisbury Friendship Club, Qld Australia, with their loyal friendship quality in mind as an inspiration.

Ample well-wishing I send today,

Hearty prayer for the world with care, for
Each and everyone out there,
Again and again I declare.
Love Divine is on the way,
Innermost loving thoughts underway,
Necessary healing energy to convey
Glory to the world every day.

Perpetual prayers in earnest,
Releasing their energy fast,
Attune to the Divine I must,
Yes, for the wisdom of prayer to grasp,
Easy to do this task, for
Redemption I humbly ask.

Healing prayers

Finally it is clear,
On with a healing prayer to spear,
Restoration of body and mind so dear.

Then and there I rejoice and cheer,
Healing on the way to revere,
Essential for happiness to domineer.

Wade in vigorously I do, and ask an
Overflow of blessings to come fast, I
Reclaim my Divine right and appeal
Lovingly to the Holy within to reveal
Divine healing, and the bliss of peace to thrill.

Dutifully I dwell
Instantly Divine healing to swell,
Vengeance to repel,
Inspiring, loving thoughts instead,
Nasty illness to dispel,
Envisaging it never to return.

Harmonious thoughts and words
Entering and swarming in my inner world,
Always and for as long as I know
Limitations to overthrow.
In their place, free spirit to grow,
Non-stop to propel,
Gloriously to excel.

Receiving kindly, with respect,
Energy Divine, abundantly I expect,
Conceive and accept,
Endless healing to maintain,
Inside of my domain.
Vehemently I proclaim, to
Emerge victorious and gain
Divinity again to reign.

Healing prayers

Winsome healing energy flows
Inevitably from the tips of my toes,
To the top of my head it grows,
Heavenly big, body and mind restored.

Graciously I infuse energy Divine,
Replenished and rejuvenated I thrive,
Alive and transformed to be precise,
Cherished body and mind revived,
Each day to cheer and contrive.

Gladness in my heart
Ready to play the part,
Accessing inner wisdom is a start.
Thought awareness to assert,
In so far as I have a head start.
Thankful for the Divine healings,
Unseen healthy feelings
Delightfully reveal and reflect
Endless trust and respect.

Faith and hope is a must
Opportunities come fast
Regardless of the task.

Turning point in delight,
Health restored outright,
Evidently everything is alright.

Healing prayers

Devotion to healing prayer
Invigorates my soul to prepare, for
Vitality to flare, that
Immensely I cherish with care.
No more no less, divine healing soars,
Ever so body, mind and soul restores.

Heightened feelings galore, soul
Elevation I do not ignore,
Abundance of health I adore,
Luck is pouring for sure
In its entirety, for me to know
Never mind what was before,
Glorious life I am thankful for.

Loving thoughts always on my mind,
Onward marching with time,
Vigorously, desiring healing to find,
Inner peace and Divine wisdom to guide.
Nightly I pray and behold,
Graciously my health is restored.

Today and every day
Happily I pray.
Overflow of warm feelings on display
Unfailing, to come to me night and day,
Generously the Divine will obey.
Heart and soul do crave
Thought healing energy to be underway.

Radiance all around is awesome,
Emerging from the core of Thyself.
Swiftly flows and restores,
Time and again outpours,
Out of nowhere bestows,
Realigning body and soul
Ever to feel whole,
Sincere loving thought gives power to uphold.

Happily I continue with my life,
Eagerly feeling alive, to
Attract what I imagine and desire.
Life enjoyable I admire,
Tranquility within and no excuse,
Holiness found and that's good news.

Stefka Harp

This is the moment to love and dwell, and
Hence every other moment as well,
Endlessly, it's a promise I tell. On

Waking up I see the light and yell,
Overwhelmed I am with love to propel.
Ready for loving emotions to ignite, as
Dedication to love stamps out evil outright.

Indefinite! Love and The Word are dynamite, I
Surrender to love with a strong appetite.

Lifelong commitment to the Holy to domineer
On and on for eternity is quite clear.
Verify I do, to love tirelessly and persevere.
Enforce it I do, fervently, and revere.

Healing prayers

Hocus pocus,
Ever so I focus
Adamantly on the pain,
Lovingly it's for my gain,
Tremendous healing for body and brain
Heavens above, now I am okay.

Passionately, with all my might, I
Repent and send love overnight, to the
Almighty who art in heaven,
Yes, in his own garden,
Enthroned eternally,
Reigning supreme, our Holy, indefinitely.

Gladness in my heart,
Rise and shine I do to start
Anew over again,
Consciously, health to maintain
Each and every day,
Ferociously within my domain
Ultimate aim is
Lovingly good health to regain.

Hard and fast continuously
Empowering ardently,
Amazingly, without delay
Leading to happy days,
Invigorating heart and soul to praise
Night and day without phase
Glorious healing energies ablaze.

Healing prayers

Unfailingly I do it for myself and the world,
Propelling spiritual growth,
Obviously I am fortunate
Now and forever to have spiritual attainment.

Yes, the prayer is to ignite,
Overflow of health to be in sight,
Utmost trust in the Divine is a delight.

At long last a task for you and me, to
Nurture body and soul with glee,
Discover the healing power of harmony

Manifesting graceful healing overnight,
Everlasting good health outright.

I gratefully praise and pray

Radiance on me is okay,
Each day is a sunray, a
Jewell in the crown on display.
Overwhelmed I am to greet the
Inspiring and vibrant Holy spirit,
Calm, serene and profound,
Endless health wrapped around.

Invigorated I am you see,
Now and forever, cheerfully.

Tender loving care each day,
Happily I do it as I play,
Eminently forever on display.

Healing prayers

Remarkably my health is here to stay,
Empowered in every way,
Simple as that,
Through and through, and not a sweat.
Old ways of thinking I
Renounce, and cast out the
Energy that brought the ill around. Now I
Delight in the health found.

Hooray! Joyful times ahead of me,
Extraordinary happy events to see, the
Answer to my plea,
Lively and free.
The time of my life I revere,
Health and happiness domineer.

I know God never asks anything, but to

Love him with all my heart is everything.
One way to be connected
Vigorously I am commanded and protected
Enemies to be loved and respected.

The Word is Love in his kingdom,
Hence, Love is the Word in all wisdom, soul
Elation and holiness is my vision.

For all I know His Excellence wants me to
Always love and nothing else. It is
The only emotion that propels,
Heavenly stamping out evil and farewells,
Ensuring even when I am not aware,
Restless and with burden to bear.

Today and every day, God is there
He loves me I declare,
Every time I mess up he takes care.

Spirit of love and strength comes cheerfully,
Openly speaks to me, gleefully,
Nothing else but truth, wisdom and harmony.

And reminds me to love my neighbours like
None other, but as myself and family members
Dear Jesus, my love and trust is to be remembered.

The Lord teaches me how to be strong his way, I
Humbly submit to the Almighty and praise
Each day and ask for holiness always.

Help me God to walk by the Word, to
Overcome destructive feelings, Lord, my
Love for you is pure as a dove,
Yearning to keep my heart calm. And if I

Stray, whisper your love in my ear
Protect me from my carelessness sphere,
If my actions, thoughts and words are
Reckless and out of sorts,
Indeed forgive me, redemption is my reward,
The Word is Love, Truth and spiritual growth.

Passionately for healing I plead,
Repetition of healing prayers with speed, for
All my thought energies to exceed.
Yearning for powerful Divine protection,
Energising body and brain without question,
Restoring and healing with perfection.

From the tips of my toes, all
Over to the top of my head goes
Rejuvenating energy that everyone knows,

Ample healing energy flows.

Healing prayers

Hopeful I am with my pursuit,
Enthused to say the least,
Amplifying healing energy to assist,
Leaping ahead to persist, for
The body, illness to resist.
Heavenly well wishes in earnest
Yes, for Divine healing I insist.

Beaming with joy overfilled,
Onward only until, the
Day I am healed,
Yielding healthy body in a Divine shield.

Tribute to you Lord, who art in heaven,
Hallowed be your name and your Chosen,
Ever your kingdom comes, for which I am gladdened.

Lovingly your will be done
On Earth as it is in heaven.
Ray of hope on the count of seven,
Day in and day out we are strengthened, as
Supply of our daily bread is given.

Dear lord, forgive our trespasses as we ask,
In an instant, as we forgive others fast.
Vindicate those who trespass against us,
Infinite protection from evil at a glance,
Not to lead us into temptation, while
Eternally we ask for redemption.

Paramount is good health and faithfulness,
Radiance, love and happiness,
Adherence to hope, faith and holiness,
Yielding Divine righteousness.
Eternally glorified your Highness, our
Reverence, pure love and gratitude to you always.

I have come to know

Love is the only way to go,
Overall truth to follow,
Vibrant loving thoughts to bestow,
Enemies to love for evermore.

Magnificent way to be living,
Your universal Love Divine to be giving,

Essential it is for peace to find.
Nasty thought energies are unkind, but
Endless loving thoughts will nullify.
Meanwhile love energy will purify,
Inner peace and calm will amplify.
Empowered I am and unified,
Sincere thought energy glorified.

Healing prayers

Praiseful I am and obey at ease, in
Regard to loving my enemies,
Affectionately, I dare say,
Yielding protection, keeping evil at bay,
Every day bringing a sunray,
Rewarded by health and safety I daresay.

I pray for Divine healing and

Do not stop until I get the healthy feeling
Event that meets my needs.
Signalling my thought energies,
In no way can fail or displease, to
Remedy what's been lost, yielding
Excellent health at no cost.

Desire fulfilled in all fairness
I know, in no time for sure,
Victory galore, to
Inspire and overawe,
Nothing less than health and happiness
Every day and for evermore.

Healing prayers

Haste is not my way to turn,
Expressing emotions is not an issue,
Ascertaining my needs is a breakthrough,
Loyalty at my best.
Inner peace reigns supreme,
Nifty way to start the day
Gratifying and glorious I would say.

The ultimate outcome is
Obvious, no matter what, I

Farewell the ills through a prayer
Immediately, and no scare
Night or day I dare,
Delightful healing I find, I declare.

Perpetual prayers without excuse,
Rejuvenation they infuse,
Attention from the Holy I seek,
Yearning truth to know and speak,
Evermore life abundant to pour,
Ready to take me furthermore,
Sublime to the core.

Almighty, hear my plea
Rectify all the wrongs with glee,
Endow me with health and harmony.

Healing prayers

Priority is health for me and my family,
Our safety and welfare clearly.
Watch over us closely,
Everlasting endeavour, you do with glory.
Redemption we ask for, and that's our story.
Furthermore wisdom galore,
Utmost awesomeness we implore,
Love Divine we adore.

At the end of the day, it's
Time to rest and reflect.

Trace my thoughts and recognise
Hard and fast I need to repent and apologise, if
Earthly peace is to come before sunrise.

Eager to start the day afresh and awake,
Nothing but the best to bake,
Desires fulfilled, it's a piece of cake.

Healing prayers

Over and again I praise and pray, for
Forgiveness and safety every day.

Thanking the Divine in earnest,
Humbly for my family safety I ask,
Every step of the way in God I trust.

Displaying diligence is wise,
Awareness of thoughts likewise,
Yes, health and wealth I visualise.

Remarkable are body and soul
Embraced as a whole,
Joyful moment to know and uphold.
Unconditional love is the goal
Veraciously sent out to the world.
Empowering others is a pot of gold,
Never mind what kind, it is
Always to remind,
Tenderly to be on my mind, to be
Immersed with the Divine.
Outflow of rejuvenation to find
Now, will be a good time.

Peaceful nature of mine,
Radiant, generous and wise,
At long last I shine.
Youthful body, mind and soul combined,
Essential to be aligned,
Rejuvenated, thrilled and Divine.

Glorious healing prayer should be
Rather fast I agree,
Acceleration without doubt,
Carefully sent out,
Endless well-wishing beauties.
Forward only those energies to
Undo the wrong and dispel, with
Love, ill health, and evil to repel.

Happy soul, healthy body without argue, I
Enjoy the graceful healing that is my due,
Allowing me happily to continue through.
Lack of loving thoughts can undo, so
I inspire loving thoughts whatever I do.
Notably I start anew,
Grateful for healing thoughts to pursue.

Glorious, yet another day Lord,
Order of the Holy in accord,
Opportunity to be loved and adored,
Delightful, good night's sleep restored.
Nightly I praise and pray for
Infinite Divine protection to come my way.
Gratitude for my safety, my family and the world,
Happiness all along,
Temptation to resist and evil to overthrow.

Priceless to have a good night's sleep,
Rejuvenation softly creeps.
Another day, happily I accept
Your Almighty loving whisper with respect.
Every moment I live is an awesome conquest,
Renewed body and soul I caress.

Stefka Harp

I send out with all my might a

Selection of healing prayers in delight.
Equally if it's no help outright, it's
Not going to bring harm overnight.
Divine healing energy released

Over time, hopefully has increased to
Undo the wrongs and align with
The Divine, desired healing to find.

At long last I assign

Harmless healing prayers to send away,
Effortlessly night and day. I
Acquired the habit to say them aloud,
Loud as I can and proud,
In tune with heart and soul to guide
Non-stop, passionately to bind
Gently, Divine healing energy with time.

Healing prayers

Passionately with all my heart, a
Ritual that makes the sound of a harp.
Attention I give to my prayer,
Yes, every detail, showing I care.
Each thought and word could begin to
Restore body and soul within.

Earthly prayer sent out to fulfill,
Very real it is to overfill
Energy to heal,
Rejuvenation for the mind to instill,
Youth and vibrance, such a thrill.

Dedication to healing prayers galore,
Always and for evermore,
Yearning for healing to flow.

Stefka Harp

About the author

Stefka was born during World War II in a small village tucked away in the foothills of a big mountain in Eastern Macedonia.

Her family, like others in the village, gained their food from the land. It was a self-sufficient household. This lifestyle built much confidence in her and her siblings.

She migrated to Australia in 1972, where she still resides. She finished her degree, and a diploma in counselling, and gained jobs in the welfare sector.

The last seven years before she retired were spent supporting those who experienced domestic violence. While working with people, she used her knowledge of the power of thought as a creator of our destiny. She has seen astonishing improvements when people change their attitude and implement positive and loving thoughts. Prayer, forgiveness, hope and faith go hand in hand with positive growth and attitudes.

Academic achievements

Diploma of Community Services Management
 Southbank Institute of TAFE 2006

Diploma in Counselling
 Australian Institute of Counsellors 1993–1994

Bachelor of Arts Degree (Major Psychology)
 University of Queensland 1989

Economics, book keeping & accounting
 Business Studies College (Macedonia)

www.ingramcontent.com/pod-product-compliance
Lightning Source LLC
Chambersburg PA
CBHW061251040426
42444CB00010B/2356